DAVID S. LAROSA

Hailo Raspberry Pi 5 User Guide

A comprehensive manual to unlock the new features of this single board computer with the Hailo-8L Module and all you need to know

Contents

Introduction

With the Hailo-8L AI module with the Raspberry Pi 5, welcome to a new era of computing. Whether you're a seasoned developer or a curious novice, this tutorial aims to help you realize the full potential of these robust tools.

The single-board computer industry has advanced significantly with the release of the Raspberry Pi 5. With more flexibility, better visuals, and processing power, it opens up a world of possibilities for a variety of applications, from simple tasks to intricate systems. The Raspberry Pi 5's integration with the Hailo-8L AI module, which puts cutting-edge artificial intelligence capabilities at your fingertips, is what really makes it stand out.

The Hailo-8L AI module is a state-of-the-art AI accelerator that turns the Raspberry Pi 5 into a powerful AI powerhouse. It was created by the creative Israeli company Hailo. The Hailo-8L gives the Raspberry Pi 5 the ability to do 13 tera-operations per second (TOPS), which is more than enough for handling complex AI tasks like object detection and real-time video processing. Because of this, it's the perfect platform for AI-driven projects as well as edge computing applications.

Everything you need to get started with your Raspberry Pi 5 and Hailo-8L AI module is covered in this extensive guide. We will go over the fundamentals of configuring the Hailo-8L module and installing the required software on your Raspberry Pi 5. You will discover the basic ideas behind artificial intelligence (AI) and machine learning, as well as how to use well-known frameworks like TensorFlow, PyTorch, and OpenCV to implement these technologies.

We will also look at a range of real-world AI projects, ranging from camera-based ones like facial recognition and object detection to non-camera ones like speech recognition and automated smart homes. We explore advanced subjects including maximizing AI performance and integrating the Raspberry Pi with other devices for individuals who want to push the envelope.

Case studies and success stories from the real world will inspire and enlighten readers about the variety of uses for the Raspberry Pi 5 and the Hailo-8L module. We will also provide advice on how to keep your setup up to date and solve frequent problems so that your projects function without a hitch.

You'll learn how much potential there is when you combine the Raspberry Pi 5 with the Hailo-8L module as you go on this adventure. With this tutorial, you will hopefully get the knowledge and abilities necessary to design creative and significant AI projects for your own use, your career, or the benefit of the larger tech community.

Using the Raspberry Pi 5 and the Hailo-8L module, let's explore the fascinating field of artificial intelligence and discover how you may bring your ideas to life.

Greetings from the Raspberry Pi 5 Future of AI.

The Raspberry Pi series has completely changed the computing industry by enabling everyone, from professionals to amateurs, to own a powerful, reasonably priced, and adaptable single-board computer. The incorporation of powerful artificial intelligence (AI) capabilities with the Hailo-8L Module has allowed for even more options since the release of the Raspberry Pi 5.

- The Raspberry Pi 5 Overview

The Raspberry Pi 5 is a major improvement over its predecessors, with more powerful CPU, better graphics, and a modular design that makes adding specialist parts easier. This model advances not just in terms of its inherent hardware capabilities but also in terms of its capacity to accommodate contemporary computing requirements, such as AI and machine learning applications.

- Overview of the Hailo-8L Module

The Raspberry Pi ecology is transformed with the Hailo-8L Module. The Raspberry Pi 5 now has unmatched AI inferencing capabilities thanks to this module, which was created by Hailo, an Israeli company known for its edge AI processors. The Hailo-8L, with its capability of 13 tera-operations per second (TOPS), enables sophisticated artificial intelligence applications, such as object detection and real-time video processing, on a small and power-efficient platform.

- Objective and Coverage of This Guide

The goal of this article is to give readers a thorough grasp of how to utilize the Hailo-8L Module in particular to unleash the full potential of the Raspberry Pi 5. This book will walk you through every step, whether you are an experienced developer trying to incorporate AI into your projects or a novice excited to learn about the newest advancements in computer technology. You'll discover comprehensive instructions, helpful hints, and motivational projects that highlight the potential of this potent combo, covering everything from unboxing and configuring your Raspberry Pi 5 to implementing cutting-edge AI applications.

Chapter 1: Getting Started with Raspberry Pi 5

A major turning point in the development of single-board computers is the Raspberry Pi 5. The Raspberry Pi 5 builds on the success of its predecessors by adding a plethora of new features and improvements that make it more capable, adaptable, and user-friendly than before. A plethora of opportunities for learning, experimenting, and creativity are presented by the Raspberry Pi 5, regardless of one's role: hobbyist, instructor, student, or professional developer.

We'll walk you through the first steps of setting up your Raspberry Pi 5 in this chapter. We will cover every necessary detail, from unpacking your new gadget to setting it up for the first time, to make sure you have a seamless and successful setup process. You will be prepared to explore the boundless potential of this amazing tiny computer and enter into the thrilling world of Raspberry Pi projects by the end of this chapter.

To assist you understand the purpose of each component and how it fits together, we will first take a closer look at the ones that arrive with your Raspberry Pi 5. After that, we'll guide you through setting up your device for the first time, including attaching any peripherals and turning it on. In order to provide you a strong base on which to grow, we will finally walk you through the process of installing the Raspberry Pi OS, which is the suggested operating system for your Raspberry Pi 5.

Starting with a Raspberry Pi 5 is a thrilling adventure that offers lots of chances to develop, learn, and create. Whether you are upgrading from an earlier model or configuring a Raspberry Pi for the first time, this chapter will provide you with the information and assurance you need to get the most out of your new machine. Now let's begin and take the Raspberry Pi 5 on this thrilling journey.

Opening the Box and Configuring the Raspberry Pi 5

The initial phase in delving into the realm of single-board computing involves opening the packaging of your Raspberry Pi 5. We'll walk you through the process of unboxing and configuring your Raspberry Pi 5 in this part. Everything you need to start your Raspberry Pi journey will be provided, from figuring out which parts are in the package to connecting peripherals and turning on your device. Now let's take a closer look at what's inside your Raspberry Pi 5 package.

Overview of Components

Your Raspberry Pi 5 will come per-assembled with all the parts you need to get going when you receive it. The following is what to anticipate from the box:

The Raspberry Pi 5 board
  Energy source
  HDMI connections and a Raspberry Pi OS reloaded on a microSD card
  USB cords
  Not required: Hailo-8L Module (if acquired in a kit)
  - Basic Setup

Linking the Elements:

Place the MicroSD card into the Raspberry Pi's slot located on its underside.
   Attach the Raspberry Pi's HDMI cord to your monitor.
   Connect the mouse and keyboard via USB.
   After plugging the Raspberry Pi's power supply into the outlet, disconnect
it.
   Initial Boot:

The Raspberry Pi will boot into Raspberry Pi OS when it is powered up.
   To configure your language, time zone, and network options, adhere to the
on-screen directions.

Setting up the Raspberry Pi OS

- Installing and getting the OS ready

For best speed and security, even though your MicroSD card is preloaded,
you might wish to install the most recent version of Raspberry Pi OS.

Get the Raspberry Pi Imager here:

Get the Raspberry Pi Imager for your operating system by going to the official
Raspberry Pi website.
   Get the MicroSD card ready:

Put the MicroSD card inside your PC.
   Choose the most recent Raspberry Pi OS version when you launch the
Raspberry Pi Imager.
   From the list of storage devices, select the appropriate MicroSD card.
   To begin the installation procedure, click "Write."

- A Comprehensive Installation Guide

Put the MicroSD card in place:

Take the MicroSD card out of your computer and place it into your Raspberry Pi after the installation is finished.

Link and Activate:

After connecting the keyboard, mouse, and monitor, turn on the Raspberry Pi.

First Configuration:

To configure system settings, including creating a user account and establishing a Wi-Fi connection, follow the basic setup prompts.

Revise the Framework:

The following commands should be entered into the terminal to make sure your system is up to date:

```
sql
  sudo apt update
  Sudo apt-full-upgrade
```

Now that your Raspberry Pi 5 is operational, you can begin experimenting with its features and begin integrating the Hailo-8L Module.

Chapter 2: Exploring the Hailo-8L Module

A major turning point in the development of single-board computers is the Raspberry Pi 5. The Raspberry Pi 5 builds on the success of its predecessors by adding a plethora of new features and improvements that make it more capable, adaptable, and user-friendly than before. A plethora of opportunities for learning, experimenting, and creativity are presented by the Raspberry Pi 5, regardless of one's role: hobbyist, instructor, student, or professional developer.

We'll walk you through the first steps of setting up your Raspberry Pi 5 in this chapter. We will cover every necessary detail, from unpacking your new gadget to setting it up for the first time, to make sure you have a seamless and successful setup process. You will be prepared to explore the boundless potential of this amazing tiny computer and enter into the thrilling world of Raspberry Pi projects by the end of this chapter.

To assist you understand the purpose of each component and how it fits together, we will first take a closer look at the ones that arrive with your Raspberry Pi 5. After that, we'll guide you through setting up your device for the first time, including attaching any peripherals and turning it on. In order to provide you a strong base on which to grow, we will finally walk you through the process of installing the Raspberry Pi OS, which is the suggested operating system for your Raspberry Pi 5.

Starting with a Raspberry Pi 5 is a thrilling adventure that offers lots of chances to develop, learn, and create. Whether you are upgrading from an earlier model or configuring a Raspberry Pi for the first time, this chapter will provide you with the information and assurance you need to get the most out of your new machine. Now let's begin and take the Raspberry Pi 5 on this thrilling journey.

Opening the Box and Configuring the Raspberry Pi 5

The initial phase in delving into the realm of single-board computing involves opening the packaging of your Raspberry Pi 5. We'll walk you through the process of unboxing and configuring your Raspberry Pi 5 in this part. Everything you need to start your Raspberry Pi journey will be provided, from figuring out which parts are in the package to connecting peripherals and turning on your device. Now let's take a closer look at what's inside your Raspberry Pi 5 package.

Overview of Components

Your Raspberry Pi 5 will come pre-assembled with all the parts you need to get going when you receive it. The following is what to anticipate from the box:

The Raspberry Pi 5 board
   Energy source
   HDMI connections and a Raspberry Pi OS preloaded on a microSD card
   USB cords
   Not required: Hailo-8L Module (if acquired in a kit)

- Basic Setup

Linking the Elements:

Place the MicroSD card into the Raspberry Pi's slot located on its underside.
   Attach the Raspberry Pi's HDMI cord to your monitor.
   Connect the mouse and keyboard via USB.
   After plugging the Raspberry Pi's power supply into the outlet, disconnect it.
   Initial Boot:

The Raspberry Pi will boot into Raspberry Pi OS when it is powered up.
   To configure your language, time zone, and network options, adhere to the on-screen directions.

Setting up the Raspberry Pi OS

- Installing and getting the OS ready

For best speed and security, even though your MicroSD card is preloaded, you might wish to install the most recent version of Raspberry Pi OS.

Get the Raspberry Pi Imager here:

Get the Raspberry Pi Imager for your operating system by going to the official Raspberry Pi website.
   Get the MicroSD card ready:

Put the MicroSD card inside your PC.
   Choose the most recent Raspberry Pi OS version when you launch the Raspberry Pi Imager.

From the list of storage devices, select the appropriate MicroSD card. To begin the installation procedure, click "Write."

- A Comprehensive Installation Guide

Put the MicroSD card in place:

Take the MicroSD card out of your computer and place it into your Raspberry Pi after the installation is finished.
    Link and Activate:

After connecting the keyboard, mouse, and monitor, turn on the Raspberry Pi.
    First Configuration:

To configure system settings, including creating a user account and establishing a Wi-Fi connection, follow the basic setup prompts.
    Revise the Framework:

The following commands should be entered into the terminal to make sure your system is up to date:

```sql
sudo apt update
Sudo apt-full-upgrade
```

Now that your Raspberry Pi 5 is operational, you can begin experimenting with its features and begin integrating the Hailo-8L Module.

Introducing the amazing world of the Hailo-8L Module, a cutting-edge addition to the Raspberry Pi ecosystem that unlocks previously unheard-of AI powers. We take a thorough look at the Hailo-8L Module in this chapter, going over all of its features, capabilities, and possible uses.

The Hailo-8L Module, which offers remarkable performance and efficiency in a small form factor, represents a substantial development in AI technology. This module, which is made to work seamlessly with the Raspberry Pi 5, uses the Hailo-8L AI accelerator to power a variety of AI-driven tasks and projects.

We'll explore the main characteristics and advantages of the Hailo-8L Module as we set out on this exploration, learning how it expands the capabilities of the Raspberry Pi 5 and gives users the ability to explore uncharted territory in AI creation. We'll explore every aspect of this revolutionary technology, from installation to compatibility with current Raspberry Pi software stacks, to fully grasp its potential.

Come explore the world of the Hailo-8L Module with us, where creativity is unrestricted and artificial intelligence is just around the corner. Let's explore this ground-breaking module's core and learn about the countless opportunities that lie ahead.

Highlights of the Hailo-8L Module

Fans of the Raspberry Pi, get ready for a revolutionary addition to the always changing single-board computer landscape. We are proud to present the Hailo-8L Module, a revolutionary AI accelerator that has been painstakingly designed to push the capabilities of the Raspberry Pi 5 to previously unheard-of levels.

The result of constant innovation and state-of-the-art technology is contained within the little, ground-breaking module. The Hailo-8L Module, created in partnership with Israeli chipmaker Hailo, offers an astounding 13 tera-operations per second (TOPS) of inferencing performance, marking a quantum leap forward in edge-based AI processing.

Fundamentally, the goal of the Hailo-8L Module is to enable both seasoned experts and budding innovators to fully utilize artificial intelligence in their projects. This curriculum opens up new possibilities for creativity and ushers in a new era of intelligent edge computing, whether you're interested in robotics, computer vision, or natural language processing.

However, the Hailo-8L Module's real beauty is found in its smooth interaction with the Raspberry Pi environment as well as in its unadulterated computing capability. When combined with the most recent Raspberry Pi 5, this module becomes the central component of AI-driven projects, opening up a vast array of possibilities for both developers and hobbyists.

In the chapters that follow, we'll delve deeper into the complexities of the Hailo-8L Module, revealing its inner workings and countless uses, and plotting a route for an AI-powered future without limits. Come along on this thrilling adventure with us as we set out to maximize the Hailo-8L Module's capabilities and push the limits of what is conceivable with the Raspberry Pi.

Principal Elements and Advantages

Emblematic of innovation, the Hailo 8L Module offers an array of state of-the-art features and advantages that propel it to the forefront of AI acceleration technology. Let's examine some of its most important qualities and all the advantages it offers:

1. Unmatched Performance in Inferencing:

The Hailo-8L Module, with its remarkable 13 tera-operations per second

(TOPS) of inferencing capability, raises the bar for edge-based AI processing. It is perfect for applications needing quick decision-making because of its blazingly fast computations, which allow real-time analysis of data streams.

2. Small Dimensions:

- The Hailo-8L Module's small form factor and powerful processing capabilities allow it to be seamlessly integrated into a variety of hardware setups. Because of its small size and flexible deployment, it can be used in areas with limited space.

3. Effectiveness of Energy Use:

By utilizing sophisticated architecture and optimization methods, the Hailo-8L Module attains exceptional energy economy, using a minuscule amount of power in comparison to conventional AI accelerators. This energy-efficient design lowers environmental effect while also cutting operating costs.

4. Flexibility in Compatibility:

- The Hailo-8L Module was created with flexibility in mind and can be used with a wide range of platforms and devices, including the Raspberry Pi 5. The development process is made simpler by its smooth interface with current technology, which enables quick prototyping and implementation of AI-driven solutions.

5. Adjustability and Adaptability:

- Engineered to support a broad spectrum of use cases, the Hailo-8L Module's scalability and flexibility allow developers to customize its performance to meet particular application needs. This module offers robotic control, speech recognition, and object detection the processing ability to handle a wide range of jobs.

6. Forward-Looking Design:

With a focus on the future, the Hailo-8L Module features a future-proof architecture that accounts for changing AI workloads and advances in technology. Long-term viability is ensured by its modular architecture and upgradability, which make it possible to seamlessly integrate any future improvements and optimizations.

7. Ecosystem Friendly to Developers:

- To go along with its hardware prowess, Hailo has a robust developer environment that includes tools to speed up development, SDKs, and extensive documentation. To easily expedite their AI projects, developers can access a multitude of tools, such as community forums, sample code, and tutorials.

In conclusion, the Hailo-8L Module, which combines unparalleled performance, energy efficiency, and versatility in a small container, is the epitome of edge-based AI acceleration. This ground-breaking module gives you the ability to push the limits of intelligent edge computing, whether you're starting a new AI project or looking to improve current applications.

- Installation Manual

It's easy to install the Hailo-8L Module and guarantee perfect interaction with your Raspberry Pi 5 configuration. To begin, adhere to these detailed instructions:

Step 1: Assemble the Required Tools

Make sure you have the following supplies available:
   - Hailo-8L Module - Raspberry Pi 5 single board computer - Required wires and connectors

Step2: Get Your Raspberry Pi 5 Ready

- Turn off your Raspberry Pi 5 and unplug all attached accessories.
    - Find the Raspberry Pi 5 board's M.2 slot. Usually, it is situated close to the board's edge.
    - If required, take off any shields or coverings to reveal the connector in the M.2 slot.

Place the Hailo-8L Module in Step 3.

- Make sure the Hailo-8L Module is positioned carefully in the M.2 slot on your Raspberry Pi 5 board.
    - Make sure the connectors are seated correctly by carefully inserting the module into the slot.
    - Press firmly to lock the module into position.

Step 4: Keep the Module Safe

- Use the M.2 module mounting screws that come with your Raspberry Pi 5 board to firmly attach the Hailo-8L Module.
    - Gently tighten the screws to avoid damaging the Raspberry Pi 5 board or the module.

Step 5: Put Your Raspberry Pi 5 Setup Back Together

- After the Hailo-8L Module is firmly in place, turn on your Raspberry Pi 5 and reconnect any peripherals.
    - Assume that your Raspberry Pi 5 boots up successfully by following the regular procedure.

Step 6: Check the Installation

- Once your Raspberry Pi 5 has started up, make sure the Hailo-8L Module is detected and operating as intended.

- The operating system on your Raspberry Pi allows you to view the system information and use the command line interface to see if the module is present.

Installing software and drivers is step seven (if necessary).

- To fully utilize the features of the Hailo-8L Module, you might need to install extra drivers or software, depending on your particular use case and software requirements.

- For guidance on installing the required drivers and software components, refer to the documentation that either your software vendor or Hailo provides.

Step 8: Use Hailo-8L to begin investigating AI

- Now that the Hailo-8L Module has been installed successfully, you may use your Raspberry Pi 5 to investigate the fascinating field of artificial intelligence.

- With Hailo-8L, explore AI frameworks, create creative projects, and realize the full potential of edge-based AI computing.

You may quickly and simply install the Hailo-8L Module and start using its potent AI capabilities with your Raspberry Pi 5 configuration by following these easy steps. I hope you have fun exploring the world of intelligent edge computing!

Chapter 3: AI and Machine Learning Basics

A major turning point in the development of single-board computers is the Raspberry Pi 5. The Raspberry Pi 5 builds on the success of its predecessors by adding a plethora of new features and improvements that make it more capable, adaptable, and user-friendly than before. A plethora of opportunities for learning, experimenting, and creativity are presented by the Raspberry Pi 5, regardless of one's role: hobbyist, instructor, student, or professional developer.

We'll walk you through the first steps of setting up your Raspberry Pi 5 in this chapter. We will cover every necessary detail, from unpacking your new gadget to setting it up for the first time, to make sure you have a seamless and successful setup process. You will be prepared to explore the boundless potential of this amazing tiny computer and enter into the thrilling world of Raspberry Pi projects by the end of this chapter.

To assist you understand the purpose of each component and how it fits together, we will first take a closer look at the ones that arrive with your Raspberry Pi 5. After that, we'll guide you through setting up your device for the first time, including attaching any peripherals and turning it on. In order to provide you a strong base on which to grow, we will finally walk you through the process of installing the Raspberry Pi OS, which is the suggested operating system for your Raspberry Pi 5.

Starting with a Raspberry Pi 5 is a thrilling adventure that offers lots of chances to develop, learn, and create. Whether you are upgrading from an earlier model or configuring a Raspberry Pi for the first time, this chapter will provide you with the information and assurance you need to get the most out of your new machine. Now let's begin and take the Raspberry Pi 5 on this thrilling journey.

Opening the Box and Configuring the Raspberry Pi 5

The initial phase in delving into the realm of single-board computing involves opening the packaging of your Raspberry Pi 5. We'll walk you through the process of unboxing and configuring your Raspberry Pi 5 in this part. Everything you need to start your Raspberry Pi journey will be provided, from figuring out which parts are in the package to connecting peripherals and turning on your device. Now let's take a closer look at what's inside your Raspberry Pi 5 package.

Overview of Components

Your Raspberry Pi 5 will come pre-assembled with all the parts you need to get going when you receive it. The following is what to anticipate from the box:

The Raspberry Pi 5 board
  Energy source
  HDMI connections and a Raspberry Pi OS preloaded on a microSD card
  USB cords
  Not required: Hailo-8L Module (if acquired in a kit)

- Basic Setup

Linking the Elements:

Place the MicroSD card into the Raspberry Pi's slot located on its underside.
   Attach the Raspberry Pi's HDMI cord to your monitor.
   Connect the mouse and keyboard via USB.
   After plugging the Raspberry Pi's power supply into the outlet, disconnect it.
   Initial Boot:

The Raspberry Pi will boot into Raspberry Pi OS when it is powered up.
   To configure your language, time zone, and network options, adhere to the on-screen directions.

Setting up the Raspberry Pi OS

- Installing and getting the OS ready

For best speed and security, even though your MicroSD card is preloaded, you might wish to install the most recent version of Raspberry Pi OS.

Get the Raspberry Pi Image here:

Get the Raspberry Pi Imager for your operating system by going to the official Raspberry Pi website.
   Get the MicroSD card ready:

Put the MicroSD card inside your PC.
   Choose the most recent Raspberry Pi OS version when you launch the Raspberry Pi Imager.

From the list of storage devices, select the appropriate MicroSD card. To begin the installation procedure, click "Write."

- A Comprehensive Installation Guide

Put the MicroSD card in place:

Take the MicroSD card out of your computer and place it into your Raspberry Pi after the installation is finished.
Link and Activate:

After connecting the keyboard, mouse, and monitor, turn on the Raspberry Pi.
First Configuration:

To configure system settings, including creating a user account and establishing a Wi-Fi connection, follow the basic setup prompts.
Revise the Framework:

The following commands should be entered into the terminal to make sure your system is up to date:

```sql
sudo apt update
Sudo apt-full-upgrade
```

Now that your Raspberry Pi 5 is operational, you can begin experimenting with its features and begin integrating the Hailo-8L Module.

The fields of machine learning (ML) and artificial intelligence (AI) have moved from science fiction to useful, real-world applications in recent years.

Professionals and hobbyists alike now need to understand the foundations of AI and ML because these technologies are still transforming a wide range of sectors and industries.

Fundamentally, artificial intelligence (AI) is the computer systems' imitation of human intelligence processes. It includes a broad range of methods and strategies intended to provide machines the ability to carry out operations like perception, learning, problem-solving, and decision-making that normally need human intelligence. As a branch of artificial intelligence, machine learning focuses on creating models and algorithms that let computers learn from data and get better over time without needing to be explicitly programmed.

We will explore the fundamentals of AI and ML in this chapter, giving a synopsis of important ideas, jargon, and techniques. This chapter provides a thorough introduction to the fascinating field of AI and ML, covering everything from comprehending the principles of neural networks to investigating well-known AI frameworks like TensorFlow, PyTorch, and OpenCV. This chapter will provide the foundation for your journey into the field of intelligent computing, regardless of your level of experience. From beginners looking to understand the basics to seasoned professionals looking to expand your knowledge.

Knowing Machine Learning and Artificial Intelligence

We explore the foundational ideas of machine learning (ML) and artificial intelligence (AI) in this chapter. It is essential to comprehend these ideas since they serve as the foundation for the projects and applications that we will discuss later in this tutorial. We'll begin by deciphering the fundamental concepts and language of AI and ML, giving you a strong basis on which to understand the complexities of these cutting-edge technologies. Together with the Raspberry Pi 5, let's set off on this trip to unleash the promise of AI and ML.

- Foundational Ideas and Terminology

Understanding the fundamental ideas and jargon in the fields of artificial intelligence (AI) and machine learning (ML) is similar to learning a new language. It is imperative that we become familiar with important concepts and core principles in order to efficiently navigate the environment of AI and ML.

Fundamentally, artificial intelligence (AI) is the replication of human intellect in machines, allowing them to carry out activities like perception, decision-making, and problem-solving that normally need human intelligence. As a branch of artificial intelligence, machine learning focuses on creating algorithms that let computers learn from data and make judgments or predictions without explicit programming.

As we dig more, we come across other ideas that are essential to ML and AI, such as:

1. An algorithm is a collection of guidelines or instructions created to carry out a certain task or solve a certain problem.

2. Data: The unprocessed information that machine learning and artificial intelligence algorithms utilize to learn and make judgments. There are many different types of data, such as unstructured data (text, photos, videos), and structured data (arranged in a certain way, like databases).

3. Models are made using algorithms that have been trained on data and serve as representations of actual systems or processes. Using fresh incoming data as a basis for predictions or choices, models are employed.

4. Training: The act of providing data to an ML model so that it can identify trends and connections. The model modifies its parameters during training in order to reduce errors and boost efficiency.

5. A sort of machine learning technique known as supervised learning uses labeled data—that is, pairs of accurate outputs for each input—to train the model. By mapping inputs to outputs according to the supplied labels, the model gains the ability to anticipate outcomes.

6. Unsupervised Learning: Algorithms for unsupervised learning are learned on unlabeled data, in opposition to supervised learning. Without explicit guidance, the model has to find patterns and relationships in the data.

7. A computational model called a neural network is based on the composition and operations of the human brain. Neural networks are made up of layers of interconnected nodes, or neurons, and they have the ability to learn intricate patterns from data.

8. A feature is a specific, quantifiable attribute or quality of an observed occurrence. Features are crucial inputs for machine learning models and have the power to affect the model's output.

Gaining an understanding of these fundamental ideas and terms paves the way for investigating more complex AI and ML subjects and starting real-world Raspberry Pi 5 projects.

- An Introduction to Neural Networks

Artificial intelligence's cutting edge is represented by neural networks, which use data to predict outcomes and solve complicated problems by imitating the structure and operation of the human brain. Neural networks are fundamentally made up of layers of connected nodes, or artificial neurons. Every neuron in the network takes in input signals, processes them, and outputs an output signal that other neurons in the network can use as input.

The perceptron is the fundamental unit of a neural network. It accepts numerous input values, multiplies each by a weight, adds up the weighted inputs, and then applies an activation function to get an output. The procedure is then repeated with the following layer of neurons receiving this output. Neural networks have the capability to estimate complex functions and generate precise predictions by manipulating the weights and biases of individual neurons.

Based on their structure and patterns of connectivity, neural networks can be divided into several categories:

1. Feedforward Neural Networks (FNNs): Information passes between hidden nodes and output nodes in a single direction in FNNs. Regression and classification tasks are appropriate for these networks.

2. Recurrent Neural Networks (RNNs): RNNs are able to display dynamic temporal activity because of their directed cycle-forming connections. Sequential data processing activities like as time series prediction and natural language processing are ideally suited for them.

3. CNNs, or convolutional neural networks, are made to handle structured, grid-like data, like pictures. They are very useful for applications like object and picture detection because they use convolutional layers to automatically learn spatial hierarchies of characteristics from the input data.

4. Generative Adversarial Networks (GANs): GANs are made up of a discriminator and a generator neural network that are trained concurrently via adversarial learning. GANs are utilized in applications such as image production and data augmentation, and they can produce new data samples that mimic the training data distribution.

Neural networks have achieved state-of-the-art performance on multiple benchmark tests, revolutionizing fields like speech recognition, computer vision, and natural language processing. In the age of big data and artificial intelligence, they are essential tools due to their capacity to recognize intricate patterns in data and extrapolate those patterns to previously unobserved instances. As we learn more about neural networks, we open up new avenues for technological innovation and advancement.

Creating AI Frameworks

Creating artificial intelligence frameworks is an essential first step in using AI for a variety of applications. AI frameworks offer the libraries and tools required to effectively create, train, and implement machine learning models. TensorFlow, PyTorch, and OpenCV are some of the most widely used AI frameworks; they each have special features and capabilities to meet various requirements.

1. TensorFlow: An open-source machine learning framework created by Google Brain, TensorFlow is renowned for its scalability, adaptability, and vast tool and resource ecosystem. TensorFlow offers high-level APIs for simple model construction and deployment, and it supports both conventional and deep learning machine learning models. Developers may create and train neural networks with TensorFlow for a variety of applications, including as reinforcement learning, natural language processing, and picture classification.

2. PyTorch: Known for its user-friendly programming interface and dynamic computational graph, PyTorch is a potent open-source machine learning platform. PyTorch, a neural network construction tool developed by Facebook's AI Research team, provides a more imperative and Pythonic approach, facilitating experimentation with various model structures and

methods. PyTorch is extensively utilized in fields including healthcare, finance, and autonomous driving for research, prototyping, and production-level deployments.

3. OpenCV (Open Source Computer Vision Library) is a popular open-source library for computer vision tasks, despite not being a standard machine learning framework. For processing images and videos, OpenCV offers an extensive collection of tools and algorithms for tasks like object tracking, feature detection, and camera calibration. While not being a deep learning specialist, OpenCV easily interacts with frameworks like as TensorFlow and PyTorch, enabling developers to combine deep learning models with conventional computer vision techniques for more reliable and accurate outcomes.

Installing the required software dependencies, like Python and CUDA (for GPU acceleration), and setting up the development environment are usually involved in setting up these AI frameworks. Once installed, developers can take advantage of these frameworks' broad functionality and copious documentation to create intelligent applications that push the limits of artificial intelligence. In the quickly changing world of machine learning and artificial intelligence, knowing how to use AI frameworks is crucial for anybody working in research, data science, or software engineering.

- Overview of OpenCV, PyTorch, and TensorFlow

The choice of frameworks is crucial in the field of artificial intelligence and machine learning as it shapes the application development process and its final products' capabilities. Three notable pillars in this environment are TensorFlow, PyTorch, and OpenCV; each provides a distinct set of features and benefits to meet a range of demands and preferences.

TensorFlow: Created by Google Brain, TensorFlow has become a major force in the machine learning and deep learning fields. Its large ecosystem, scalability, and solid design make it an excellent option for projects ranging from research to production-level work. Because of TensorFlow's versatility, programmers may create and train a wide variety of neural networks, from straightforward feedforward networks to intricate convolutional and recurrent designs. High-level APIs like Keras make model construction and deployment easier, allowing for quick experimentation and iteration. TensorFlow's scalability and performance are further enhanced by its support for hardware accelerators like GPUs and TPUs, as well as distributed computing. This makes it an excellent choice for handling challenging machine learning jobs.

PyTorch: Created by Facebook's AI Research group, PyTorch is a popular tool because of its easy-to-use syntax, dynamic computational graph, and smooth Python integration. PyTorch takes a more imperative approach than TensorFlow, which makes it possible to create dynamic computation graphs and easily debug them. Because of its adaptability, PyTorch is especially well-suited for research and experimentation, allowing developers to quickly and easily change model structures and algorithms as needed. Researchers can train sophisticated neural networks more quickly and effectively because to PyTorch's robust support for autograd and GPU acceleration. Its large library of pre-trained models also helps developers create innovative AI applications more quickly.

With its extensive collection of tools and algorithms for processing images and videos, OpenCV (Open Source Computer Vision Library) is a mainstay in the field of computer vision. OpenCV provides a diverse collection of functions to address a wide range of computer vision difficulties, from simple tasks like image resizing and filtering to complex ones like object detection and facial recognition. Developers working with different programming languages can utilize it thanks to its C++ and Python interfaces, and its cross-platform compatibility guarantees a smooth integration with a range of environments and systems. OpenCV is not a deep learning framework in and of itself, but it is a useful addition to TensorFlow and PyTorch since it provides conventional computer vision methods that can improve the robustness and performance of deep learning models in practical settings.

To summarize, machine learning and computer vision professionals need to have three essential tools in their toolbox: TensorFlow, PyTorch, and OpenCV. These frameworks offer the information and building blocks you need to realize your ideas, whether you are researching deep learning, developing AI-powered applications, or investigating computer vision. Gaining expertise in TensorFlow, PyTorch, and OpenCV will help you realize your full potential in developing intelligent systems that push the envelope of creativity and bring about revolutionary change in a variety of fields and businesses.

- Illustrative AI Projects

Exploring artificial intelligence (AI) brings up a world of possibilities where cutting-edge technology and creative ideas come together to tackle pressing issues and bring about revolutionary change. This section explores a wide range of sample AI projects that demonstrate the adaptability and potential of AI across different fields and applications.

1. Identification and Detection of Objects:

- Basic tasks in computer vision, object detection and recognition have applications in everything from driverless vehicles and augmented reality to surveillance and security. TensorFlow and PyTorch are two deep learning frameworks that developers can use to train convolutional neural networks (CNNs) to recognize and categorize objects in pictures and videos. Developers can perform real-time object identification on the Raspberry Pi 5 by utilizing pre-trained models like YOLO (You Only Look Once) or SSD (Single Shot MultiBox Detector). This opens up applications such as intelligent robots, object tracking systems, and smart surveillance cameras.

2. Pose Approximation and Facial Spatial Reference:

- Applications like gesture recognition, human-computer interaction, and biometric identification are made possible by computers' ability to comprehend the spatial arrangement and structure of human bodies and faces thanks to pose estimation and facial landmarking. Developers can train posture estimation models to identify important body joints and face landmarks from pictures and videos by using deep learning techniques and libraries such as OpenCV. Developers can create interactive applications such as virtual try-on systems, fitness tracking gadgets, and emotion detection tools by integrating these models with the Raspberry Pi 5 and the Hailo-8L module.

3. Speech Recognition:

- Speech recognition technology makes it possible for computers to translate spoken words into text, opening the door for applications like voice-activated gadgets, virtual assistants, and speech-to-text systems. Developers can train recurrent neural networks (RNNs) or transformer models to recognize and comprehend spoken instructions and conversations by utilizing deep learning frameworks such as TensorFlow and PyTorch. Through the integration of speech recognition models with the audio input capabilities of the Raspberry Pi 5 and the accelerated processing power of the Hailo-8L, developers may create intelligent voice-enabled applications for communication, accessibility, and home automation.

4. Automation of Smart Homes:

- Smart home automation systems improve comfort, convenience, and energy efficiency in residential settings by utilizing AI and IoT (Internet of Things) technology. Developers may design intelligent systems that automate domestic chores, optimize energy use, and provide residents customized experiences by leveraging machine learning algorithms and sensor data. Through the integration of AI models with the Raspberry Pi 5 and Hailo-8L, developers may incorporate functionalities like voice-activated appliances, predictive maintenance, and adaptive lighting, thereby converting standard houses into intelligent and networked environments.

3. Speech Recogniti

Chapter 4: Maintenance and Troubleshooting

To guarantee the seamless functioning of your AI projects powered by Raspberry Pi 5 requires proactive maintenance and efficient troubleshooting techniques. This chapter covers the best methods for keeping your system up to date and fixing typical problems that can crop up during development and deployment.

1. Tips for Routine Maintenance:

Maintaining the functionality and dependability of your Raspberry Pi 5 with Hailo-8L module requires routine maintenance. It's crucial to carry out regular maintenance on your system, including cleaning, software updates, and system health monitoring.

- Cleaning: Over time, dust and debris may build up on the Raspberry Pi 5 board and Hailo-8L module, which may cause overheating and a decline in performance. To get rid of any accumulation, regularly check and clean the components using a soft brush or compressed air.

- Software Updates: Keep your Raspberry Pi OS, Hailo-8L drivers, and AI frameworks up to date with the most recent updates. Install updates when you see them to guarantee compatibility, security, and performance gains.

- System Monitoring: Using the built-in tools or external monitoring software, keep an eye on the Raspberry Pi 5 system's temperature, CPU and memory utilization. To avoid system crashes or slowdowns, keep a watch on resource-intensive tasks and take quick action to correct any anomalies.

2. Common Problems and Their Fixes:.

- When using the Raspberry Pi 5 and Hailo-8L, you could run into a number of problems even with careful planning and upkeep. You can overcome obstacles and complete your tasks on schedule by being aware of frequent problems and troubleshooting methods.

- Overheating: A typical problem with Raspberry Pis and other small form-factor computers is overheating. To avoid overheating, make sure the Raspberry Pi 5 board and Hailo-8L module have enough ventilation and airflow around them. If required, think about utilizing heatsinks or active cooling solutions.

- Power source Issues: System breakdowns and unpredictable behavior might result from an inadequate or unreliable power source. Employ a top-notch power source that can give enough voltage and current to run your Hailo-8L module and Raspberry Pi 5. Power adapters that are of poor quality or that are counterfeit should not be used as they might not produce power consistently.

- Software Compatibility Problems: Runtime failures and instability may result from incompatibilities between the Hailo-8L drivers, AI frameworks, and the Raspberry Pi OS. Make sure the software components and libraries you're utilizing are compatible with each other. Refer to the official documentation and community forums for updates and troubleshooting tips.

- Connectivity Problems: Problems with networking and connectivity may prevent your Raspberry Pi 5 system from communicating with outside services or devices. To verify correct connectivity, check your router settings, cables, and network configuration. Use the diagnostic tools and commands included in the Raspberry Pi OS to troubleshoot network problems.

These maintenance advice and troubleshooting approaches will help you get the most out of your Raspberry Pi 5-based AI projects in terms of performance, dependability, and lifetime. To fully realize the potential of your AI inventions, be watchful, proactive, and resourceful when handling maintenance responsibilities and finding solutions.

Keeping Your Configuration

Thorough upkeep and tactical management are necessary to guarantee the smooth functioning of your Raspberry Pi 5-based artificial intelligence initiatives. In this section, we take a look at the basic procedures that are necessary to maintain the effectiveness and dependability of your system. We explore the essentials of caring for your Raspberry Pi 5 and Hailo-8L module, from basic maintenance to preventative measures, so you may confidently and skillfully support your AI projects. Together, let's set out on this adventure to protect the quality and functionality of your creative works.

- Tips for Routine Maintenance

1. Physical Inspection: Keep an eye out for any indications of physical damage, loose connections, or overheating on your Raspberry Pi 5 and Hailo-8L module. To avoid any possible problems, make sure that every part is firmly fastened and adequately ventilated.

2. Software upgrades: Make sure you are utilizing the most recent firmware and software upgrades for your AI frameworks and libraries, as well as the Raspberry Pi OS. Frequently, these upgrades come with security patches, bug fixes, and speed enhancements that are necessary for the best possible functionality.

3. Backup Data: To protect your important data and configurations, put in place a regular backup plan. You may promptly recover from any unanticipated data loss or corruption by keeping a trustworthy backup, regardless of whether it's project files, trained models, or system settings.

4. Monitor System Resources: To keep tabs on system resources like CPU, RAM, and storage capacity, use monitoring tools. You can find any resource shortages or bottlenecks before they affect performance by keeping an eye on these measures.

5. Clean Air Vents: An collection of dust and debris can obstruct airflow and cause problems with overheating. To ensure ideal thermal performance and stop component deterioration over time, clean the air vents and fan (if applicable) on a regular basis.

6. Inspect Power Supply: Verify that the power supply unit (PSU) is providing a steady and sufficient amount of electricity to your Raspberry Pi 5. Inadequate power or fluctuations can lead to system instability and possible component damage. Think about utilizing a top-notch PSU with enough voltage regulation and power output.

7. Examine Logs: To spot any irregularities or possible problems, routinely examine system logs and error messages. Log files can give you important information about error circumstances, system behavior, and performance patterns, enabling you to proactively resolve any underlying problems.

You can guarantee the lifespan, stability, and peak performance of your Raspberry Pi 5-based artificial intelligence projects by according to these routine maintenance guidelines. This will free you up to concentrate on exploration and creativity rather than worrying about the dependability of your system.

- Software Upgrades and Typical Problems
    Updates for software:

Maintaining the smooth and secure operation of your Raspberry Pi 5 with Hailo-8L module requires regular software upgrades. Bug fixes, security patches, and performance enhancements that contribute to better system operation and stability are often included in these updates. Here's how to efficiently handle software updates:

1. Update Procedure: Learn how to update the Raspberry Pi operating system and any installed software packages. Updates can be carried out with the 'apt} package management, graphical update tools, or automatic scripts, depending on your system.

2. Scheduled Updates: Make sure you have a regular timetable for updating and monitoring your software. To make sure you are aware of the most recent updates and security fixes, think about setting up automated update checks and notifications.

3. Make a backup of your system before updating: To guard against possible data loss or system corruption, it's a good idea to make a backup of your system before installing any software updates. To take a snapshot of your present system configuration, use disk imaging software or backup tools.

4. Check Updates: After installing software updates, spend some time making sure the system is operating properly. Verify that there are no regressions or compatibility problems after the update by testing important functionality, apps, and services.

Typical Problems:

Although the Raspberry Pi 5 and Hailo-8L are strong devices, users may occasionally run into problems that need to be troubleshooted and resolved. The following common problems and solutions are listed:

1. Boot Failure: Verify the integrity of your SD card, power supply, and

hardware connections if your Raspberry Pi is unable to boot up or displays error messages during startup. Ascertain that the SD card is correctly inserted, has a valid operating system image on it, and that the power source is supplying enough voltage and current.

2. Overheating: If the Raspberry Pi 5 and Hailo-8L module are exposed to excessive computing demands or insufficient airflow, overheating may transpire. Using the built-in tools or third-party software, keep an eye on the system's temperature. To enhance thermal dissipation, think about installing heatsinks or cooling fans.

3. Compatibility Issues: Make sure that the operating system version and Raspberry Pi architecture are compatible with any software packages, libraries, or AI frameworks you install. If you run into problems with compatibility or dependencies, look for newer versions or alternatives that are supported by the community.

4. Networking Issues: Try troubleshooting common networking components including switches, routers, cables, and wireless adapters if you're having problems connecting to the network. To find and fix connectivity problems, check firewall rules, DHCP configuration, and network settings.

5. Peripheral Compatibility: Make sure your Raspberry Pi 5 is compatible with the peripherals you connect, including cameras, sensors, or displays, and that the operating system supports them. Consult the manufacturer's specifications and community forums to obtain information on compatibility and troubleshooting techniques.

You can preserve the efficiency, stability, and dependability of your Raspberry Pi 5-based AI projects and guarantee a flawless user experience by being vigilant about software upgrades and swiftly resolving typical problems.

Conclusion: The Future of AI with Raspberry Pi 5

As we come to the end of this thorough tutorial on using the Raspberry Pi 5 and the Hailo-8L module to harness the power of AI, it's important to consider the ramifications going forward and possible developments in this fascinating field. The combination of state-of-the-art AI acceleration technology and reasonably priced single-board computing opens up a world of possibilities for professionals, developers, and hobbyists alike.

- New Developments in Edge Computing and AI

The rise of edge computing, where data processing and analysis take place closer to the source of data collection, is one of the major factors influencing AI's future. Individuals and companies may take advantage of strong AI capabilities right within their embedded systems, Internet of Things devices, and edge computing settings using the Raspberry Pi 5 with the Hailo-8L module. For AI-driven applications, this approach offers real-time decision-making, decreased latency, and improved privacy and security.

- The Next Course of Action for Fans and Developers

There has never been a better moment to investigate and experiment with AI technologies on the Raspberry Pi platform, as AI keeps growing and becoming more and more integrated into our daily lives. The Hailo-8L module with the Raspberry Pi 5's accessibility and affordability offer a compelling opportunity for anybody, be it a hobbyist, student, entrepreneur, or experienced developer, to innovate and create AI-powered solutions across a varied range of domains.

The following actions are things to think about when you start using AI and the Raspberry Pi 5:

1. Constant Learning: Maintain your curiosity and stay up to date on the most recent advancements in edge computing, AI, and machine learning. To increase your knowledge and abilities, look through community forums, tutorials, and online resources.

2. Project Exploration: Using the Raspberry Pi 5 and the Hailo-8L module, set a challenge for yourself to take on new AI projects and applications. Try your hand at robots, computer vision, natural language processing, and other AI-driven fields to see how your imagination and problem-solving skills can be used.

3. Collaboration and Networking: To work together on AI projects and exchange knowledge and experiences, connect with like-minded people, become a member of your local maker community, and take part in hackathons and workshops. Peer networking can offer insightful perspectives, encouragement, and motivation for your pursuits.

4. Community Contribution: Make your initiatives, ideas, and lessons known to the larger Raspberry Pi and AI community. Encourage a culture of cooperation and knowledge sharing by writing tutorials, mentoring newcomers, and contributing to open-source projects.

You have the chance to be at the forefront of innovation and change in the field of embedded AI computing by embracing the future of AI with Raspberry Pi 5. Whether you're developing intelligent gadgets, investigating AI-powered applications, or pushing the limits of technology, the Raspberry Pi 5 gives you the ability to influence AI's direction and have a significant global impact.

www.ingramcontent.com/pod-product-compliance
Lightning Source LLC
Chambersburg PA
CBHW061055050326
40690CB00012B/2628